A STAR IN THE SEA

A STAR IN THE SEA

by

ALVIN and VIRGINIA SILVERSTEIN

illustrated by SYMEON SHIMIN

Frederick Warne and Company, Inc.
New York and London

For Laura Donna Silverstein

Sunlight sparkled on a shallow pool in a rocky hollow just beyond the edge of the sea. A month ago there had been no pool there at all, for the lapping waves of the restless ocean usually did not reach so far.

But one night there had been a violent storm. Torrents of rain poured down. Giant waves lashed the shore. It was the huge waves that filled the little tidal pool and left in it many sea creatures. There were fish of different sizes, shapes and colors. There were many-legged crabs, hard-shelled clams and mussels, spiny sea urchins and starfish. There were soft-bodied, flower-like sea anemones and sea lilies with gently waving tentacles.

After the storm, the new little pool settled down. The creatures stranded there took up life again as they knew it on the ocean bottom. Small fish darted in and out of the green jungle of seaweed, nibbling hungrily and hiding from larger fish that snapped at them. Sometimes one of the little fish swam too close to a flower-like sea anemone—an animal with deadly stingers. Then the anemone stunned the little fish, and its waving tentacles pulled the helpless victim to its waiting mouth.

Scurrying along the bottom were crabs, hunting for food. Near them, moving very slowly, were two bright purple starfish. The starfish were not searching for food, for it was their breeding season and one was a male, the other a female.

Suddenly a milky white cloud of tiny eggs—millions of them—burst into the water from small openings in the female's body. The male starfish answered her with his own cloud, but his was made up of millions of sperm. The clouds mixed. One by one sperm found eggs and the pairs joined to begin the lives of new baby starfish.

It might seem strange that mating starfish send so many eggs and sperm into the water. And it is true that if each sperm found an egg, the pool would soon be filled with millions of baby starfish. But it never happens that way. Many sperms never find eggs. Even when an egg and a sperm have been lucky enough to find each other, all may not go well. In the peaceful-seeming water dangers lurk everywhere. A fish might gobble down a whole swarm of baby starfish in a single mouthful. Or a water current might take some unknowing baby starfish right into the mouth of a hungry sea anemone.

Though many starfish were born in the small world of the tidal pool, not many would survive. Let us follow the life of one of the lucky ones. Her name is Stella.

The tiny starfish eggs floated in the water. Each was so small that we could not even have seen it without a microscope. But there were many—millions of them.

Some of the eggs had never found a sperm and would soon die. But others had been fertilized— they had met and joined with a precious seed from a male starfish, and now marvelous changes were taking place. Inside each fertilized egg, chemicals were shifting back and forth, forming new ones and breaking down old ones. Some of these wonderful chemicals held blueprints, plans for how a new starfish would grow and live. And little by little a small creature was taking shape— following its blueprints step by step.

The fertilized egg that was one day to grow into Stella divided into two cells, which stayed clinging together like two tiny balls. The two cells became four, and then eight, and so on, until Stella had grown to be a small swimming creature.

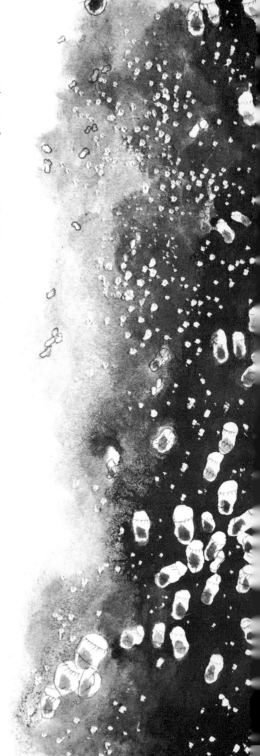

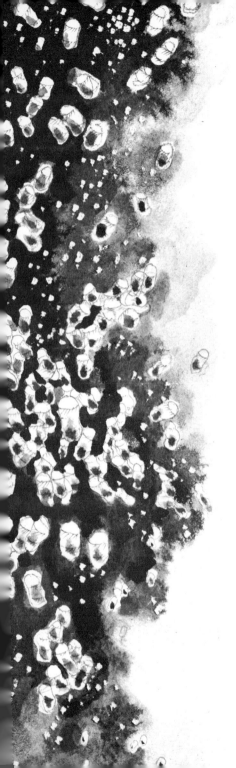

If we had looked at Stella then (we would still have needed a microscope to see her well), we would have been quite surprised. For she did not look like a starfish at all! She looked like a knobby little bean, and she swam about in the water near the top of the pool with rows of little hairlike "oars," called cilia, which beat back and forth like the oars of an ancient ship.

Stella swam and floated about in the water of the pool, feeding on even smaller single-celled bits of plant life. Scattered through the pool were other baby starfish like Stella. Scientists would call them larvae, like the larvae of bees and butterflies and other insects—young forms that will have to go through a wonderful change before they grow to look like their parents.

But where were Stella's parents? They were crawling about somewhere on the bottom of the pool, with never a care for their growing brood. For baby starfish are on their own from the very first. Many of them are eaten by other sea creatures, as were many of Stella's brothers and sisters. But a few survive and grow.

13

Weeks passed and Stella grew larger and larger. Still she did not look like a starfish. She had no starfish arms or coat of armor.

At last it was time for her magical change. Stella swam down to the bottom of the pool, found a nice smooth rock, and stuck herself to it with a little sucker near her mouth. What strange changes took place now!

Stella grew a brand-new mouth in her side, and five small arms began to grow out from her body. Many other changes took place inside her. Soon she looked like a little star, growing like a flower on a short stalk attached to the rock. When she was ready, the little starfish let go her stalk and floated away. She was now a perfect five-pointed star. But her arms were quite short and stubby, and she was still so small that she could have sat quite nicely on the head of a pin.

Now Stella stayed near the bottom of the pool. She did not swim any more. She crept along the rocks and sand. Each day she grew larger and larger. She had many narrow escapes, as fish swished close by and tried to gobble her up. But Stella always managed to disappear into a crack in the rocks or find some rock weed to hide in.

17

One day there was another great storm, even more violent than the one that had washed Stella's parents and the other sea creatures into the little pool on the shore. The sky turned black, and lightning ripped through the clouds. Sheets of rain pelted down into the small pool and stirred up Stella's little world. The water rocked violently back and forth. For a while Stella clung tightly to a rock at the bottom, anchored firmly with sucker-soled feet. She was safe.

But then the storm seemed to quiet down for a moment. The wind died away, and the water stopped its churning. Stella loosened her grip on the rock. This was a mistake. For just then a giant wave from the ocean swept in toward the shore. It swept right over and into the tidal pool —Stella's home. Stella was whisked up in the surge of water. And as the wave retreated, the little starfish was swept out to sea. She was never to return.

18

Swiftly Stella rode out to sea on the rolling wave. A moment later she was on the sea bottom. But she had fallen onto her back!

Stella had never been on her back before. She could not crawl along the rocky bottom, because her thousands of tiny sucker feet were on the wrong side—they were turned up into the water.

At first Stella tried wriggling from side to side. But this did not help. She could not flip over. Then she tried curling the tip of one of her arms backward. She stretched and strained. Now the little sucker feet at the tip of her arm were able to grip the rock. Stella held tight and pulled. Then she curled over the tips of two of her other arms as well. Now she had a good hold on the rock, and pulled herself up. For a moment she teetered back and forth, standing straight up on the tips of three of her arms. Then she flipped right over onto her sucker feet, the way she liked to be.

The storm had died away. Stella set out to explore her new home in the waters of the ocean, close to the shore. The pull of the current and the rolling of the waves did not bother her, for she made sure to keep a firm grip on the ocean bottom with some of her many sucker feet nearly all the time.

These little sucker feet were really amazing. There were thousands of them in rows down the undersides of her arms. They could hold so tightly that a strong man would have great difficulty in pulling her off a rock.

Stella found many interesting creatures on the ocean bottom, many more than she had met in her little tidal pool. There were even different kinds of starfish. Some were orange or green or brown. Although most had five arms, some had six or ten or even more. Some had long, slender arms. But others had arms so short that they just looked like points on the body of the starfish. There was even a starfish that burrowed down in the sand and rarely showed itself.

Stella found many tasty things to eat. She was getting bigger all the time, and each day she could eat larger and larger clams and mussels. One day she found an oyster bed. Stella loved oysters. They were so easy to feed on. Oysters did not move away as clams did. The oysters tried to protect themselves by keeping their shells tightly shut. But this did not stop Stella.

She would perch right on top of an oyster and clamp down firmly on its shells with her sucker feet. The oyster would try to stay closed, but Stella was patient. Steadily she pulled and pulled. At last, the oyster would grow tired and open its shell just a crack. But a crack was enough for Stella. For then she would do the strangest thing. Quick as a flash Stella would turn her own stomach inside out. She would squeeze it down so thin that it could fit through a crack no thicker than a piece of thin cardboard. Into the oyster's shell Stella would place her stomach. In a moment juices would start flowing and kill the helpless oyster.

Stella's mouth was very small. She could not fit a whole oyster inside. So she would digest the oyster right inside its own shell. Then she would suck up the tasty food, leaving behind the empty shells.

Stella loved the plump oysters and clams. Day by day she crept along the oyster bed. She was very hungry and ate one shelled creature after another. She was getting into shallow water now.

One day Stella was so busy with her meal that she did not notice a dark shadow above her. A sleek seagull plunged down through the water, straight for Stella. Before she could move, the gull seized her by one of her arms and lifted her out of the water.

Stella struggled vainly as the hungry seagull flew off with her.

As the gull flew higher, Stella wriggled and pulled. She thrashed about so much that the gull bit down with its beak harder than it meant to. Suddenly, Snap! Stella's arm broke off. The surprised gull discovered that it was holding only a single arm in its beak. Meanwhile. down, down plunged Stella to the sea below.

Splash! The little starfish was safe in the ocean. But what a price she had paid for her life. She now had only four arms.

In the days that followed, a strange and wondrous thing happened. A little bud appeared in the space where Stella had lost her fifth arm. The bud grew and took shape. It was a new arm! How lopsided Stella looked then. She had four long arms and one short one. But her new arm was growing more and more each day.

Stella was even hungrier than she had been before. She often did not have the patience to wait until she found a nice plump oyster or clam.—She ate the tiny ones. She gobbled them down whole, digested them inside her body, and then spat out the empty shells when she was finished.

25

One day, three little barnacles tried to hitch a ride on Stella's back. Some of their friends were already riding about comfortably on the backs of crabs, fish, and other animals that moved about in the sea. They got a much bigger share of the rich bits of food that drifted down through the ocean waters. But Stella did not want any free riders. As soon as the little barnacles landed on her back, tiny pincers on her skin clamped down on them and flicked them off.

The part of the sea that Stella had fallen into had many rockpiles on the bottom. One day, while she was crawling along one in search of mussels, a large codfish, feeding along the bottom, suddenly appeared. He soon noticed Stella and with a powerful lash of his tail, he turned and swam swiftly toward her. He had eaten a starfish just the day before. Now he saw a chance to catch another.

26

Closer and closer he came. Stella did not hesitate. There was a crack in the rocks near her. With her closest arm leading the way, she flowed smoothly and with surprising swiftness over the rocks, her sucker-feet gripping one after another. Into the crack she slipped—just in time.

When the cod reached the rocks, he lunged at the last tip of an arm disappearing into the rockpile. But he was too late. Angrily he lashed about. With a vicious sweep of his tail he slapped against the rockpile. Loose rocks tumbled down and buried Stella.

The cod swam about the rockpile for a while. But the starfish was not to be seen, so he darted off in search of another meal.

What had happened to Stella? Luckily none of the rocks had fallen right on her; but she was trapped. The crack in which she had hidden was covered by a wall of rocks. Stella pushed and poked. All she was able to do was loosen one small rock. But now there was a tiny hole, just large enough for one of her arms to pass through.

This was enough for Stella. She squeezed and squeezed and stretched out her whole body so that it was no thicker than a single arm. In this shape she was able to wriggle through the tiny hole.

After her narrow escape from the cod and then the rockslide, Stella was very hungry. Off she crawled looking for food. Soon she came upon a small, wriggling fish, which seemed to dangle right before her.

Stella grabbed the little fish with her arms, and holding it with her little suckers, brought it over to her mouth.

Suddenly there was a jerk, and Stella felt herself being pulled up through the water, out into the air, and onto a boat. She had been caught by a fisherman. How unhappy the fisherman was! At the first tug of the line, he thought he had caught a real fish. But it was only a starfish.

Disappointed, the fisherman took Stella off the hook and tossed her back into the ocean. Stella was disappointed too. She had lost her meal. But at least she was safe in the water again.

Soon Stella found a clam bed. Slowly she moved along the ocean bottom, eating clam after clam as she went. As the days passed, she got closer and closer to the shore. Soon she could feel the pull of the waves, passing back and forth over her. Stella continued to follow the clam bed, until she had moved almost to the edge of the water.

It was high tide, and soon the tide turned. The edge of the water moved slowly back toward the open sea. A big wave flowed into the shore and rolled back. Suddenly Stella found herself stranded on the beach.

The little starfish tried desperately to crawl back into the water. But she was quickly growing limp, and her sucker feet were not gripping very well any more. They needed water to help them work, and the water was rapidly leaking out. Stella must find some more water soon, or she would surely die.

With each passing moment the stranded starfish became more limp. The sun beat down on the quiet beach.

Stella was dying. She could no longer move and lay limply on the beach. She could last only a few minutes more without water.

Suddenly she stirred. Fresh cool water was flooding over her. Had a wave returned to save her life? Stella looked about. Her five little eyes, one at the tip of each of her arms, saw nothing. She was in a pail filled with sea water. A boy had found her on the beach, and now he was carrying her to a little pool he had found in the rocks near the shore.

As the pail bounced back and forth, Stella clung to the bottom. Her sucker feet were firm again. When the boy reached the pool, he tried to dump her into it. Frightened Stella would not let go of the pail. At last the boy turned the pail on its side and set it in the pool. Off he went to find some food for his new pet.

After the pail had lain quiet for a while in the water, Stella crawled out into the pool and began to explore. Her new home was very much like the tidal pool where she was born—except that it was much smaller. And there were very few sea creatures.

32

Soon the boy returned. He had not known what a starfish would like, so he had gathered different kinds of creatures. He had dug up some clams from the wet sand at the edge of the sea. He had caught a few crabs too. He dropped them into the pool and raced off—he was late for dinner.

The next morning the boy returned to the pool, eager to see if his new prize was still there. Sure enough, there she was, perched on a rock and eating a clam. The boy watched, fascinated, and then went back to the ocean to get her more things to eat.

Days went by, and the boy grew to know more about Stella and her way of life. He would sit for hours watching her. Each day he went to the ocean and hunted for new things to bring her.

One day the boy brought another starfish back with him, a purple one just like Stella. Eagerly he put the new starfish in the pool and watched to see what would happen. The two starfish seemed not to notice each other at all. How disappointed the boy was! He thought he had brought Stella a new friend, but she was not paying any attention at all.

34

Days passed. Then, one morning, as the boy watched, the new starfish squirted a white cloud of something through the water. Suddenly Stella lifted the tip of one arm, and then another. She seemed to sense something. A moment later she too sent a white cloud into the water. These were her eggs, and they mingled with the sperm that the other starfish had sent out into the water.

Eggs joined with sperm, and many thousands of tiny starfish started their lives in the little pool. The boy did not know this, for they were too small to see.

Weeks went by. The tiny eggs grew into starfish larvae. And because there were very few creatures in the pool that might eat them, many of the growing larvae survived. In time they fluttered to the bottom and passed through the same magical change that Stella had gone through. And now the little pool was filled with thousands of tiny five-pointed starfish, each hardly larger than the head of a pin.

Day by day they grew. Soon the boy could see them, crawling about on the rocks of the bottom.

36

He realized that these were baby starfish. They must be Stella's children. But now he had to feed not two starfish, but thousands. And soon his long vacation would be over. He would have to go home.

The boy did not know what to do. He had enjoyed the starfish family during his summer vacation. But the babies were growing bigger and bigger each day. They needed more and more food. If he left them in the pool when it was time for him to go home, they would soon starve.

The boy tried to catch the baby starfish and carry them to the sea in his pail. But he found this very difficult to do. The baby starfish, with their tiny sucker feet, held fast to the rocky bottom of the pool and refused to budge. It was hard work to pull off a single starfish without hurting it—and there were thousands of them!

What was he to do?

At last the boy had an idea. He dug a long trench down the beach, joining the pool with the sea. The ocean water lapped down the channel. Soon the pool was a part of the sea.

The boy watched as more and more of the baby starfish crawled down the trench and out to sea. Soon Stella too set out to sea.

The boy watched, sad, and at the same time, happy, for his summer friends would now be free.